NOW YOU CAN READ....
THE CHILDHOOD OF JESUS

STORY RETOLD BY ELAINE IFE

ILLUSTRATED BY ERIC ROWE

Published by Rourke Publications, Inc. P.O. Box 868,
Windermere, Florida 32786. Copyright © 1983 by Rourke
Publications, Inc. All copyrights reserved. No part of this
book may be reproduced in any form without written per-
mission from the publisher. Printed in the United States of
America.

   The Publishers acknowledge permission from Brimax
Books for the use of the name "Now You Can Read" and
"Large Type For First Readers" which identify Brimax Now
You Can Read series.

Library of Congress Cataloging in Publication Data

Ife, Elaine, 1955-
   The childhood of Jesus.

   (Now you can read—Bible stories)
   Summary: Recounts the life of Jesus from His birth to
His meeting with the teachers in the Temple of Jerusalem.
   1. Jesus Christ—Childhood—Juvenile literature.
2. Bible stories, English—N.T. Matthew.   3. Bible
stories, English—N.T. Luke.   [1. Jesus Christ—Child-
hood.   2. Bible stories—N.T. Matthew.   3. Bible stories
—N.T. Luke]   I. Rowe, Eric, 1938-   ill.   II. Title.
III. Series.
BT320.I37   1983   226'.09505   83-13809
ISBN 0-86625-223-1

GROLIER ENTERPRISES CORP.

NOW YOU CAN READ....
THE CHILDHOOD OF JESUS

On a cold, dark night, many years ago, a little baby boy was born. His mother called Him Jesus. The baby's mother was called Mary and her husband was Joseph. Shepherds from nearby and wise men from far lands went to see Jesus because He was a special Baby.

The king of the country, which was called Judea, was King Herod. He did not go to see the Baby. He was angry when he heard that Jesus was born. It was said that Jesus was to be a king when He grew up. King Herod did not want another king in his country.

He had a very cruel plan. All the little children under two years old would be killed. In that way, he could be sure that Jesus would not live.

One night, Joseph had a dream. In the dream he saw King Herod and heard his plan. Joseph knew that the Baby Jesus was in great danger. He heard a kind voice say to him, "Take Mary and the Child away from this place. Go to Egypt and stay there until it is safe."

Joseph woke up.
He put all they
needed into a bag
and he untied a
donkey.

Mary woke up too.
She lifted the
Baby Jesus and
held Him close to
her.

Then she climbed on to the donkey
and Joseph led them out of the
town.

They walked many miles until they
reached Egypt. There they lived
for a short time.

One day, Joseph heard that King Herod had died. His son had become king in his place. Joseph decided to return to his own land, but to keep away from the big towns. They made their way back to the little town of Nazareth.

There, they unpacked and tried to make their home comfortable. Rugs were laid on the floor.

Mary washed the cooking pots and ground some corn to make bread. Joseph was a carpenter. He began to make wooden tables and yokes for oxen so that he could earn a living.

In this poor, little home, Jesus grew from a Baby to a Boy. When He was about six years old, He went to school.

He learned to read and He was told stories about Moses and David. He helped Joseph to put away the tools at the end of the day.

He asked Mary and Joseph many questions. Sometimes, Mary and Joseph were surprised that Jesus knew so much.

Every year, Mary and Joseph went
with the other village people to
the big city of Jerusalem. They
joined together in a special meal.
They sang songs and said prayers
to God.

When the boys were twelve years old, they could go with their parents. Jesus was glad when He could go too.

It was a long way to Jerusalem, but at last they reached the city and made camps.

In Jerusalem, there was a large building called the Temple. Inside the Temple sat many clever teachers who read books to the people about God.

Jesus listened and talked to them for
a long time. They were surprised at
what He knew.

Jesus forgot about
Mary and Joseph.
He slept curled
up in a corner
near the walls
of the Temple
and early the
next morning,
He went inside
again.

The other people were packing up
and starting back home.

All day long they walked, stopping
at night to eat and rest.

Mary saw that Jesus
was not with them.
She ran looking
for Jesus, but she
could not find Him.
She was very
worried in case He
had been hurt.

Joseph and Mary
walked all the
way back to
Jerusalem looking
for Jesus.

"Let us go and look in the Temple," said Joseph. "That was the last place where He was seen."

They found Jesus with the teachers, talking and listening.

"We have been so worried about You," said Mary. "Why did You stay behind when we left yesterday?" Jesus said, "I thought you would know that I was in God's house and that I have His work to do."

Mary and Joseph did not know what Jesus meant, but they often thought about His words.

All these appear in the pages of the story. Can you find them?

Jesus

Mary

King Herod

Joseph

dream

Jerusalem

Temple

teachers

Now tell the story in your own words.